MW01228010

ROLL UP, ROLL UP

SHOW YOUR CANNABIS YOU CARE WITH 20 UNIQUE WAYS TO ROLL JOINTS AND BLUNTS

DANNY MALLO

DOG 'n' BONE

Published in 2014 by Dog 'n' Bone Books
An imprint of Ryland Peters & Small Ltd
20–21 Jockey's Fields 519 Broadway, 5th Floor
London WC1R 4BW   New York, NY 10012

www.rylandpeters.com

10 9 8 7 6 5 4 3 2 1

A CIP catalog record for this book is available from the
Library of Congress and the British Library.

ISBN: 978 1 909313 46 0

Printed in China

Editor: Clare Sayer
Designer: Wide Open Books
Step illustration: Dan Prange
Style illustration: John Riordan
Additional writing: Phil Gilbert

For digital editions, visit www.cicobooks.com/apps.php

CONTENTS

THE ROLLS:

INTRODUCTION

Humans began cultivating cannabis in Asia around 10,000 years ago. Since then weed has been grown in almost every environment on the planet. Its versatility and ease of cultivation made it one of the most important and widely grown crops in history. Thanks to millennia of selective breeding, plus advanced crossbreeding programs since the 1960s, the cannabis plant has developed into countless varieties and today's weed aficionado is spoilt for choice. This book is a celebration of both the variety now on offer and the huge role cannabis has played in bringing people together. Not only did it have a significant impact on the development of modern civilization, but many friendships have been forged by the hot, glowing embers of a joint. Unfortunately, as sociable as a joint may be, a standard "One-skin" doesn't go that far when shared. So for all those times when you've got a crew of smoking buddies to provide for (or if you just feel like getting extremely baked yourself!), hopefully the creations in this book will cater to your needs. Not only are some of them big enough to get a whole party high, but they're also definite conversation starters!

TOOLS
OF THE TRADE

In recent years, as recreational cannabis use has increased and its medicinal benefits are being rediscovered, head shops have appeared on most high streets and across the Internet selling a huge array of weed-related paraphernalia. From rolling papers and simple pipes to ornate glass bongs and sophisticated electronic vaporizers, these shops stock everything a stoner needs (except for the actual weed itself!). While many of the treasures found in these Aladdin's Caves of Cannabis are somewhat gimmicky and unnecessary, there are some that are essential for any master roller's collection!

ROLLING PAPERS

Papers are available in many colors, patterns, and flavors, but the two most important aspects are how it rolls and how it smokes. These depend on the size of the paper, its thickness, and what it's made from. When you first learn to roll you will probably find wide, thick papers are easier to handle and more forgiving. However, as you hone your skills, you will find the extra paper a hindrance and moving to narrower, thinner papers will lead to a superior roll and a better tasting spliff. Ultimately it's down to personal preference, but one of the most popular types of rolling paper amongst veterans are those made from pure, chlorine-free flax paper. These papers are very thin (almost transparent) but are incredibly strong.

No matter how good your papers are, sometimes you will still get a tear or a hole in your joint. If this happens, the gum strip can be cut from a rolling paper and used as a bandage. This technique is also used throughout the book for sealing the junctions of some larger joints. It's also possible to transfer the adhesiveness from one paper onto an area of another paper where there is no gum. This is particularly useful for joining papers end to end to create an extra-long paper (see page 14). Sometimes, though, especially when stoned, this can be a bit tricky and you may want to invest in a box of rip-style rolling papers. These contain a continuous length of rolling paper about 16 feet (5 meters) long!

GRINDER

The most common type, usually made from metal or plastic, consists of two cylindrical sections that join together with sharp teeth in between. Weed is put inside and the two halves turned, tearing the bud between the teeth into a fine consistency ideal for rolling.

TOBACCO

A big difference between European and US joint rollers is the use of tobacco as a mixer with weed. Europeans tend to use it, while Americans generally don't. For years, potheads on both sides of the pond have been disputing which is best. The answer is both are—they both get you high and that's the most important thing! There are, however, strong cases for both schools of thought: if your weed is slightly damp, dry tobacco can help a joint to stay alight; it makes a joint less potent (which is preferable to some who may find a pure joint too intense); and it also makes a bag of weed stretch further. On the downside, there are many health risks involved with tobacco use and smokers can easily become addicted to the nicotine.

TERMINOLOGY

Often in the United States, the word "joint" refers to a pure weed roll, while a "spliff" refers to a roll with a mix of weed and tobacco. In Europe (and this book) both words are interchangeable. Although weed can be smoked pure, hashish must be mixed with something else when rolled in a joint.

MIXING BOWL

One of the most annoying things to happen to a joint is for it to burn more down one side than the other, known as sideburning, running, or elvising. A way to avoid this, if using tobacco, is to mix your weed and tobacco first. Having some kind of small mixing bowl in your skinning-up box is much better than doing it in your hand or loose on the table top.

On a similar note: if you want to skin up outside, particularly if it is windy, take an extra baggie with you (the small grip-seal bags you tend to get weed in). Add your ground-up weed and tobacco to the baggie, breathe in a small amount of air to inflate it, seal it closed, shake it thoroughly, and then empty the smoking mix into your rolling paper.

CARD FOR ROACHES

In the US and some other parts of the world the roach refers to the butt of the joint that is left when most of it has been smoked. However, in Europe (and this book) it refers to a small piece of thin card that is rolled up and placed in the joint to act as a mouthpiece. In the US this is also known as a crutch or filter. Using a roach gives you something to hold, protects your lips from burning, prevents a build-up of tar and moisture, stops bits of the smoking mix from getting in your mouth, and means that less is wasted. Adding the roach before the roll can be tricky to begin with, but it will actually help to structure the joint and allow for a perfect fit.

HOW TO MAKE A STANDARD ROACH

Cut a piece of thin card, approximately ¾in (2cm) square. Any thin card or paper can be used but it is always best to use a piece that is unprinted, as some inks can give off toxic fumes when burned. This is where roach books are ideal; small booklets of card usually about ¾x2in (2x5cm)— the best are the plain, chlorine-free varieties. Cut the card with scissors rather than tearing it, as frayed edges can be prone to clogging up with tar. If you have to tear the card, quickly run a flame over the edges to burn away any fraying and leave a smooth finish.

Card and paper have a grain direction, just like wood, making them easier to roll in one direction than the other. If you try and roll them in the wrong direction they will keep folding at angles rather than creating a smooth curve. So first try to determine the grain and then roll accordingly between your fingers to form a small tube. Once rolled into a tube, widen one end ever so slightly, as this will help to form the conical shape of the joint.

HOW TO MAKE AN "M" ROACH

This technique is useful for making an extra-wide roach, as the folded card will prevent you from breathing in bits of smoking mix. It's also perfect for making a standard joint stand out from the crowd.

Cut a piece of suitable card about twice as long as you would for a standard roach.

Fold back a small section a little narrower than the width of roach you want.

Fold this section back on itself an equal amount.

Then fold back one more time to form an "M" shape.

To finish, roll the remaining paper around the "M."

To avoid getting a baggy section of joint next to the roach, skin up with about a third of the roach sticking out of the paper. When you've finished rolling, tap the roach in and it will help to compact the section of smoking mix next to it.

Other Useful Items

- **PDT (pokey down thing):** Used to poke down the smoking mix in the end of your finished roll. It can be any thin instrument such as a matchstick or pen.
- **Scissors and a sharp knife:** For cutting roaches and papers.
- **A needle and tweezers:** Useful for unblocking roaches and any other fiddly jobs.
- **Lots of lighters and spare lighter fuel:** Have a few available, plus some extra fuel so you don't spend the night lighting joints off the stove top when your lighter runs out!
- **Spare rolling papers:** It's 2am, the shops are closed, and your mate utters those dreaded two words… "Last paper!" We've all been there; make sure it doesn't happen again.
- **Airtight jars/pots:** To stash your bud, keep it fresh, and contain the smell. Also, keep weed in a dark place—THC decomposes in sunlight.
- **Digital scales:** A sound investment for weed buyers who want to make sure a dealer provides the correct amount.
- **More spare rolling papers:** Stash these somewhere safe ready for the time when a drink gets knocked over, turning all your other skins into papier-mâché!

STANDARD ONE-SKIN

The originator and trendsetter, this is the most important joint of them all! It doesn't matter if you are a rolling rookie or a battle-hardened rolling veteran, you must all pay homage to this the simplest and grandest of all joints. Scientists say this is the big bang of rolls! It paved the way for the other joints you will practice in this book, which all follow the same basic principles as the One-skin.

1 Take one king size rolling paper and lay it out flat with the gum at the top edge and facing toward you. If you want to use the whole paper, go straight to step 5.

2 A joint is typically rolled into a conical shape, so it's best to remove a strip of paper at a slight angle, making it narrower at the roach end. The amount of paper you tear off will depend on how fat you want your joint to be. Fold the bottom edge of the paper up so that the roach end approximately touches the center crease and the other end is up about half as much. Run your finger along this fold so that it is well flattened.

3 Lick along this folded edge to moisten the paper, being careful not to wet the paper too much. Tear away the unwanted strip and run the torn edge gently through your fingertips to smooth off any fraying.

4 Fold this torn edge up to the top edge and crease along the new fold, then unfold the paper and lay it back out flat.

5 Add a roach to your preferred side (typically the left) and fill the rest with your smoking mix. Shape the mix so that it is narrower at the roach and wider toward the other end.

6 Carefully pick up the joint with each end between a thumb and forefinger. Roll the front and back sides of the paper up and down past each other, gently pinching and pressing the mixture more and more

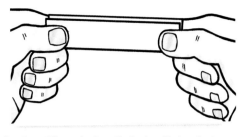

into shape, while moving your thumbs and fingers back and forth along the length of the joint to smooth out any bumps.

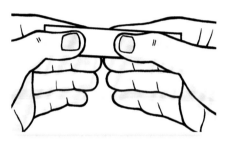

7 Use your left hand to support the roach end, while using the other hand to move from left to right, shaping the mixture into a solid cone or baseball bat shape.

8 Now for the tricky part. Roll the front edge of the paper down in line with the top of the smoking mixture and use your left thumbnail to tuck the paper in behind the roach—make sure you tuck it in as tightly as possible.

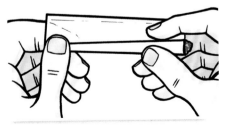

9 With the roach end still pinched between your left thumb and forefinger, support the other end with your right thumb and middle finger, while using your right index finger to run along the length of the joint, tucking the rest of the paper in behind the smoking mixture. Lick along the gum and seal the joint.

10 Tap the roach end on a hard surface and use a pen or other suitable tool to poke down the mixture inside the joint. You may also find gently rolling the joint between your thumb and fingers while tapping and poking will help smooth it out and reduce any baggy air pockets. Any smoking mixture that has fallen out along the way can now be put back in the end of the joint and poked down.

11 Twist or pinch the end, give it another little tap for luck, sit back, and spark up!

THAT'S DOPE!

You are only allowed to move onto the next joint when you have learnt to appreciate the One-skin on a Zen-like level and can roll it one-handed with your eyes closed.

When you start learning to skin up you will probably find it easier to use a whole rolling paper. As you improve, you may find standard king size papers, even the slim variety, are too wide. Removing a strip of the paper will not only make it it easier to roll but will also give a smoother smoke.

SECRET AGENT

Your mission, should you choose to accept it: roll a joint that can go undercover in the real world. This master of disguise works by hollowing out a cigarette and replacing the tobacco with smoking mix and the filter with a roach. It may sound like a simple assignment but it takes years of classified training to succeed. Once you've rolled one, put on your best Sean Connery accent and tell your friends, "The namesh Bong, Jamesh Bong, would you like to ssshmoke a ssshpliff?"

1 Gently squeeze and roll the filter end of a cigarette between your thumb and index finger. You will feel the foam filter inside becoming loose from the surrounding cigarette paper and you should be able to pull the filter out (a needle or tweezers may help here).

2 Make a roach the same width and length as the filter section and insert this into the open end of the cigarette. You may want to make a second roach and put this inside the first so that the hole is not quite so big. Alternatively, make an "M" roach (see page 7).

3 Beginning at the tobacco end and working your way up, gently squeeze and roll the cigarette between your thumb and index finger so that all the tobacco falls out.

4 Now all that's left to do is add your smoking mix to the empty cigarette, a little at a time, while poking it down along the way until it is filled and packed in tightly.

Smoke this double-O doobie and it will leave you both shaken AND stirred.

PEN METHOD

So you've failed miserably at hand-rolling a spliff but are desperate for a joint! This technique might just save the day.

1 Lay out a king size rolling paper with the gum facing toward you, then place a pencil or pen along the center crease line. If you prefer a more traditional cone-shaped joint you could make a cone out of paper or card, seal it with tape and use that instead of the pen. Alternatively, you can buy metal joint-shaped tools from most head shops that have been designed for this job.

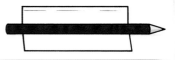

2 Pick up the paper with the pen inside, roll down the front side of the paper, and tuck it in tightly behind the pen. Lick the gum strip and then roll the pen upward with your thumbs so that the paper is sealed around the pen like a paper tube.

3 Pull the pen out of the tube of rolling paper, leaving a section of pen inside, about the same length as a roach.

4 Fill the empty paper tube with smoking mix a little bit at a time, poking it down as you go.

5 Remove the pen and add a roach in its place. Give the joint a final tap, poke, and twist off the end.

TWO-SKIN

The Two-skin is perfect for when you only have small rolling papers, or when you want a joint that lasts twice as long. This is THE social joint: great for passing to mates and big enough to make sure there's some left for you when it comes back around. Mastering the technique for joining two papers end to end is an essential skill for any expert spliff-roller, and one which will be used throughout this book.

1 Take two king size or standard rolling papers. Lay them end to end with the right one overlapping the left one by approximately the width of the gum on your papers (usually around ¼in/5mm). On the left-hand paper lick the small section of gum that will be covered by the right-hand paper and seal the two together using just this small section of gum.

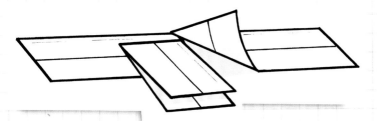

2 Take a third paper and fold it in half with its gum facing outward and moisten the gum by licking it. Place this paper in between the other two so that the moistened gum edge is lined up with the right side of the left-hand paper.

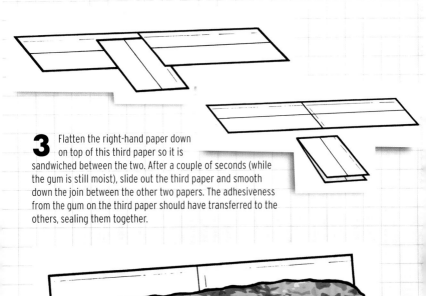

3 Flatten the right-hand paper down on top of this third paper so it is sandwiched between the two. After a couple of seconds (while the gum is still moist), slide out the third paper and smooth down the join between the other two papers. The adhesiveness from the gum on the third paper should have transferred to the others, sealing them together.

4 Add a roach and your smoking mixture. Move the smoking mixture into the rough cone shape that you want your joint to be.

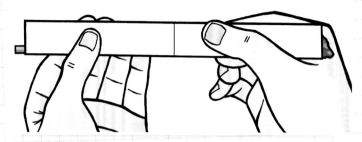

5 Rolling a joint this length is fairly tricky and you will probably find you lose half the smoking mixture out one end while you are concentrating on the other. The trick here is to support the right end of the joint on your right hand, between your thumb and forefinger. At some stages you may need to rest it as far up as your wrist. As with the One-skin joint, roll the front and back sides of the papers up and down past each other, while pinching and pressing the mixture into shape. Then, keeping your left hand at the roach end, use your right hand to move up along the joint and smooth it out. Make sure the right end is being fully supported.

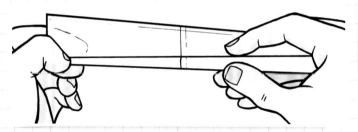

6 Bring the front edge of the paper down in line with the smoking mixture and use your left thumbnail to tuck the paper in behind the roach. Use your right forefinger to tuck the rest of the paper in behind the mixture, starting from the roach end and moving along. When you have managed to tuck the full length of the joint behind the mixture, lick the gum and seal the joint.

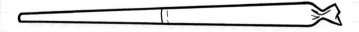

7 Give the roach end a tap, add any extra mixture that fell out during the roll, poke it all down, and twist off the end.

Twice as long and twice as strong, this jumbo joint will get you twice as stoned!

KING-L

ALL HAIL KING-L! ALL HAIL KING-L!
Get up off of your knees and find a place in court where
you can get your rolling gear out. If you want a big fat
cone of a doobie then the King-L is the joint for you.
Perfect the technique for this regal roll and it will show the
realm that you're no court jester.

1 Take two papers, typically king size; however, this method also works well when you only have small papers and fancy something a bit bigger and tastier than a small skin joint. Line them up at right angles with the gum strip at the top edge of the horizontal paper and at the left edge of the vertical paper. Lick the bottom half of the vertical paper and stick the two papers together.

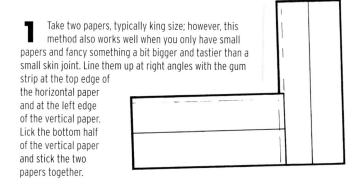

2 Fold the bottom half up to extend the horizontal crease along the full width of the L. Depending on how big and fat you want your King-L to be, you may want to tear off the top right corner of the vertical paper as the extra paper can create a harsher smoke.

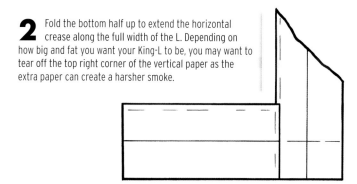

3 Add a roach to the left-hand side of the L and fill the rest with your smoking mix. Move the mix roughly into the shape you want, making the left side a little wider than the roach and the right side a few times wider.

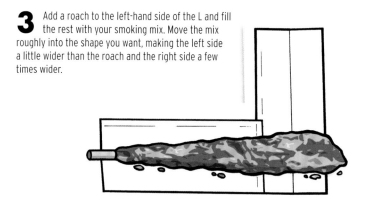

4 Pick up the L and roll the paper between your fingers to shape the mix inside into a well-formed and dense cone shape. When rolled sufficiently, the mix should retain most of its own shape.

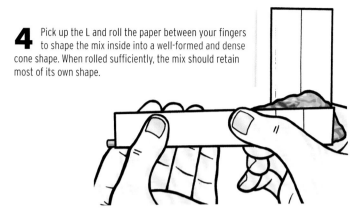

5 Using your left hand, carefully pull the front part of the paper down toward the top edge of the roach, while holding the shape of the mix together with your right hand. Use your left thumbnail to tuck the paper edge in behind the roach. Support the right end of the joint on your right hand and use your index finger to run along the top edge of the joint, tucking in the remainder of the paper. The flap of the vertical paper should be kept between the index and middle fingers for support.

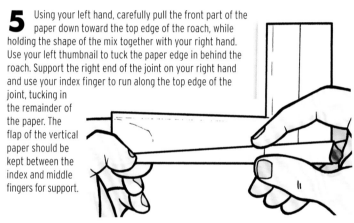

6 Once the full length of the L is tucked in, lick the gummed edge of the horizontal paper and seal it down. Now lick the gummed edge of the flap on the vertical paper and wrap it around the joint.

7 Top up the joint with any smoking mixture left over and then give it a tap, poke, and twist. There you have it, a bifta fit for a king!

MAGNUM

You've got to ask yourself a question: do I feel lucky? Well, do ya punk? If you do, then maybe you're ready to put together this bad-guy beating, fast-car chasing, roof-top jumping mega joint; aka the Magnum. It's a King-L but rolled with the upright paper at an angle so that it makes the final piece even bigger! So big that you'll have to sign a waiver to get this hand-cannon out of precinct. Once you have got this technique down, you'll have to holster up and build a forearm of steel because this is one heavy piece of artillery... only the most badass, rule-breaking mavericks out there can handle it.

1 Lay out two king size rolling papers, as shown, with the paper behind making approximately a 135-degree angle to the front horizontal paper. Lick the gum strip on the paper behind, but only the section that is being covered by the horizontal paper, and stick the horizontal paper on top of it.

2 Using scissors or by carefully tearing, remove the bottom right corner of the horizontal paper along the line that has been stuck together. Also remove the bottom part of the paper behind in line with the bottom edge of the horizontal paper.

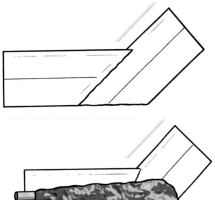

3 Add a roach to the left-hand side and fill the rest with your smoking mix. Use your fingers to move the mix roughly into the shape you want. Make the left side a little wider than the roach and the right side a few times wider. Pick up the Magnum and roll the paper between your fingers to shape the mix inside into a well-formed and dense cone shape. When rolled sufficiently, the mix should retain most of its own shape.

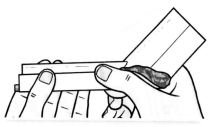

4 Using your left hand, carefully pull the front part of the paper down toward the top edge of the roach, while holding the shape of the mix together with your right hand. Use your left thumbnail to tuck the paper in behind the roach. Support the right end of the joint on your right hand and use your index finger to run along the top edge of the joint, tucking in the remainder of the paper. Support the flap of the angled paper between your index and middle fingers.

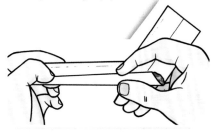

5 Once the full length of the paper is tucked in, lick the gummed edge of the horizontal paper and seal it down. Now lick the gummed edge of the flap on the vertical paper and wrap it around the joint. Top up the joint with some extra smoking mix, then give it a tap, poke, and twist.

Roll it, load it, and spin the cylinder, but be careful because, much like the recoil from a .44 Magnum, this joint kicks like a mule.

THREE-SKIN

As the saying goes, good things come in threes, and nowhere is this more true than when it comes to joints. So, all you aspiring spliff specialists, it's time for a Three-skin. This is the big bad wolf of the joint world: fat, mean, and, if you huff and puff on it for too long, your house might not get blown in but you'll certainly be pretty mashed. The structure is similar to a King-L but with an additional paper for extra width, allowing you to pack in a mountain of dope to get you, your mates, and the three little pigs nicely lean!

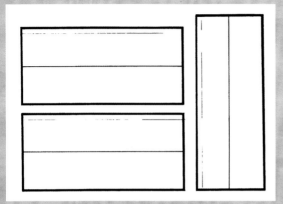

1 Flatten out three king size rolling papers, arranged as shown with the gum facing toward you.

2 Lick the gum on the bottom paper and stick it to the bottom edge of the top one. Now lick the gum on the remaining paper, but only as far along as will be needed to stick it to the other papers as shown.

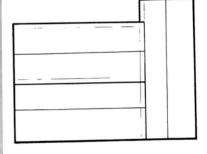

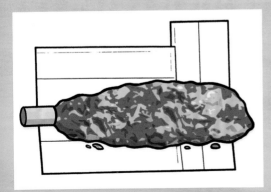

3 This joint will be very wide, like a big Cuban cigar, so you'll need to place an extra large roach at the left end of the joint. Fill the rest of the paper with plenty of smoking mix.

4 Roll the Three-skin joint in much the same way as the King-L. Move the paper between your thumb and fingers to compress the mix into a well-formed solid shape. Then

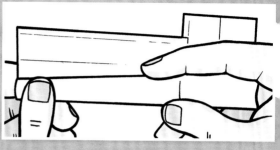

bring the front part down so that you can tuck the paper in behind the roach using your left thumbnail and the remaining paper with your right index finger.

5 Lick the gum, including the gum on the flap, and roll down. Roll and stroke between your fingers to make the joint nice and smooth, while giving it a gentle tap. Fill up any space in the end with some extra smoking mix and poke down until it's compressed and solid.

6 To prevent bits of smoking mix coming through the extra-wide roach, it is a good idea to make an additional roach, which can be put inside the first one. Alternatively, make an "M" roach (see page 7).

7 At this point it's probably a wise idea to call for some like-minded friends to come and help you enjoy this mammoth masterpiece!

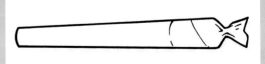

ROLL REVERSAL

Also known as the "Flaming Backflip," this is the perfect joint for showing off with. It's much trickier to pull off than it may look, so mastering this technique is the sign of a true rolling professional and will be rewarded with nods of approval from those in the know.

This method ensures that only a single layer of paper encases the joint, which provides as clean and smooth a smoke as possible. Once rolled, it is party-trick time: light the excess paper like a fuse and watch the pot pyrotechnics. It's like all the fun of a fireworks display but without having to get your feet muddy!

1 Take one king size rolling paper and lay it down so the gum is facing down and away from you. Fold the paper back on itself along the center crease.

2 With the gum still along the bottom edge and facing out, add a roach and your smoking mix. Shape the joint roughly with your fingers so it is narrower by the roach and wider toward the other end.

3 Begin to roll it in the same way you would a normal One-skin joint, moving the paper back and forth and shaping the mix between your fingers. When the joint has been sufficiently shaped and the front of the paper brought down in line with the top of the smoking mix, there are two possible options.

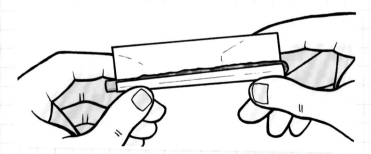

4 The gum can be licked and then tucked in behind the smoking mix, although this can be quite difficult to achieve.

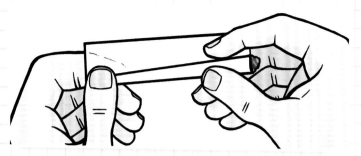

5 The alternative is to tuck the gum strip in behind the smoking mix without licking it, using your left thumbnail for the roach end and your right index finger to tuck in the rest of the paper. The gum strip will now be covered by a layer of paper but not sealed. To seal the joint you need to lick through this outer layer of paper (only where there is gum strip behind) so that the gum strip also becomes moist and sticks to the outer layer. Be careful not to lick so much that the paper becomes sodden. You should now have what looks like a One-Skin joint but with an extra flap of paper protruding from one side.

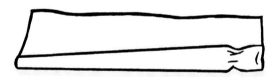

6 The extra flap of paper can now be removed. While the licked area is still slightly moist you can tear it off. However, the sign of a true professional is to light the flap at the roach end. The flames will lick up the joint and burn away the excess paper.

THAT'S DOPE!

Extra kudos can be gained by getting the roach in your mouth quick enough to take a pull at the moment the flame reaches the tip so that it effortlessly lights the joint. Just be careful you don't set your hair on fire though!

DUTCH TULIP

Pack your bags, we're off to Amsterdam—the holy land for all European joint rollers. Home to some of the most potent skunk and hash you'll ever encounter, you'll want to take a piece of it home with you. "How?" I hear you ask. The answer is: "The Tulip." This botanical beauty is a dedication to the hazy times spent in the cannabis capital, and will make your eyes even redder than the famous lights themselves.

1 Take a piece of paper or thin card, about 4in (10cm) long and 1½in (4cm) wide.

2 Roll it between your fingers to form a slightly conical tube, approximately ⅜in (8mm) in diameter at one end and ¼in (5mm) at the other. Wrap rolling papers around the tube to seal it closed. Alternatively, for an even more potent tulip, substitute this tube for a similar sized joint. However, if you're doing this, ensure the joint is a tight and solid roll that can support the weight of the tulip bud.

3 Now take two king size papers (or more if you want to make a bigger tulip). Lick the gum strip on one of the papers and stick it to the un-gummed bottom edge of the second paper to form a large rectangle. Use your hands to flatten it out.

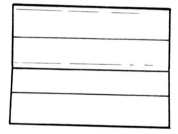

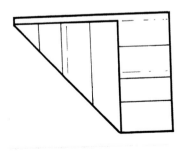

4 Fold the bottom left corner of the rectangle up at a 45-degree angle so that the edge lines up with the bottom of the gum strip.

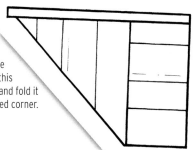

5 Without licking it, fold the gum strip down over the folded corner and run your finger along it to make a crease the full length of the paper. Fold back this crease slightly, lick the gum strip, and fold it back down so that it seals the folded corner.

6 Wait a couple of minutes for the gum to dry and then open the paper out. You should have something resembling a cone, with one side longer than the other.

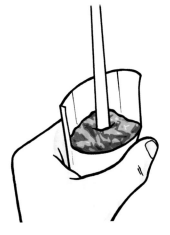

7 Fill this cone with your smoking mix and pack it down to about ⅝in (15mm) from the top. Use a pencil to gently push the mix right into the tip of the cone (be careful not to push the pencil through the paper). Now push your paper tube just into the top of the mix.

8 Using your thumb and index finger, pinch the unfilled part of the cone around the paper tube so that the mix is tightly packed into the bulb.

9 Use scissors to cut the gum strips off two or three rolling papers and wrap them tightly around the pinched part of the tulip (a piece of string or thread can be used instead).

10 Bring the loose excess flap of paper over the bulb to form the leaves of the tulip. Now get ready to enjoy the full effect of a traditional Dutch delicacy!

SNAKE BITE

Fancy a joint with a bit of venom to it? Then get your lips around a Snake Bite. Once you've smoked this slippery spliff, you'll feel like you're in a snake charmer's trance and the only known anti-venom is plenty of munchies! This reptilian reefer combines three joints in one and will teach you the important technique of using gum strips to seal any joins in your joints, a skill that will be used throughout this book.

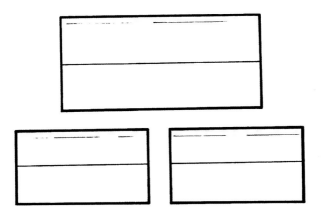

1 For this roll you will need one king size paper and two small papers, as well as a few extras for the gum strips.

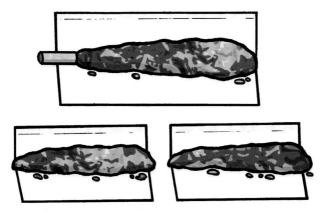

2 Prepare the king size paper as you would for a standard One-skin (see page 8), with a roach at the left and smoking mix shaped ready for rolling. Do not put roaches in the two small papers, just fill them with smoking mix all the way along.

3 Roll the joints as you would normally, tapping and poking at the end. However, only twist the ends of the small joints. Leave about ⅝in (15mm) of space at the end of the large joint and try not to compact the very last part too much. Insert the two small joints into the end of the large one.

4 Use scissors to cut the gum strips off a few extra rolling papers and stick one down through the middle of the two small joints as shown.

5 Take one or two more gum strips and wrap them around the joint, sealing it all together.

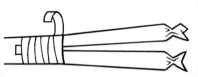

6 There it is: a snake that you want to be bitten by! Why not pack it full with some Durban Poison so its name is even more fitting?

CROSS JOINT

Made famous by Seth Rogen and James Franco in the brilliant stoner movie *Pineapple Express*. According to Franco's dope-dealing character, when lighting all three ends at the same time "the smoke converges, creating a trifecta of joint-smoking power." I don't know about that, but what I do know is this packs one hell of a punch and is more than capable of converting any non-believers of the weed! Just remember, you can't even light this thing on your own so make sure you've got a smoking buddy to help, not to mention three lighters!

1 Take one king size paper and one small paper, and lay them out with the gum facing up and toward you.

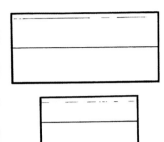

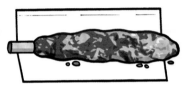

2 Add a large roach and plenty of smoking mix to the king size paper. You will need to make this joint large enough for the smaller joint to be able to pass through it. Prepare the small paper without a roach and with the smoking mix coming all the way to both ends.

3 Roll the large joint as you would a standard One-skin (see page 8) but don't compact the top half when you poke it or twist up the end too tightly; instead just pinch it closed. Roll the small joint so that it is uniform in diameter (not cone-shaped), poke both ends, and twist them.

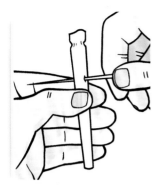

4 Take a needle, toothpick, or similar sharp instrument and poke a hole through the large joint, about two-thirds of the way up. Slowly wiggle the needle around in a circular motion to widen the hole in the joint until it looks big enough for the small joint to fit through.

5 Start to push the small joint through the hole. When it is a little way through, use the needle to make a hole through the center of the small joint to allow the air to flow through. As before, wiggle the needle to open the hole up sufficiently.

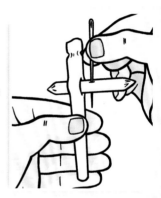

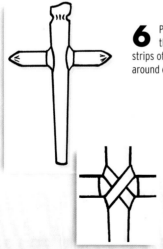

6 Pull the small joint until it is halfway through the large one. Use scissors to cut the gum strips off three or four small papers and wrap one around each of the arms of the cross to seal the gaps.

7 Use the remaining gum strips to wrap all around the junction of the cross, sealing up any remaining gaps. Smoke one of these sacred spliffs and it will give a whole new meaning to "having a hot cross bun!"

DOUBLE BUBBLE

It may look and sound like a lollipop from your childhood but I can assure you that this is a much more complex and tasty joint than even Mr Wonka himself could have dreamed up. This is the Everlasting Gobstopper of tulip joints, made with extra papers to contain the whole heap of delicious, gooey, chocolaty smoking mix within*. However, once you've smoked this tasty treat, the room may soon be filled with dancing Oompa-Loompas singing annoying, toe-tapping songs you just can't stop humming along to.

1 Take a piece of paper or thin card, about 4in (10cm) long and 1½in (4cm) wide. Roll it between your fingers to form a slightly conical tube, approximately ⅜in (8mm) in diameter at one end and ¼in (5mm) at the other. Wrap rolling papers around the tube to seal it closed.

2 Construction of the Double Bubble is similar to that of the Dutch Tulip (see page 28) but with three king size rolling papers. Lick the gum strip on one of the papers and stick it to the ungummed bottom edge of the second paper. Repeat with the third paper and stick to the bottom edge of the first two.

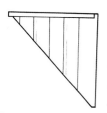

3 Fold the bottom left corner of the rectangle up at a 45-degree angle so that the edge lines up with the bottom of the gum strip. Without licking it, fold the gum strip down over the folded corner and run your finger along it to make a crease the full length of the paper.
Fold back this crease slightly, lick the gum strip, and fold it back down so that it seals the folded corner.

4 Wait a couple of minutes for the gum to dry and then open the paper out. You should have something resembling a cone.

5 Add some smoking mix to the cone (use a pencil to gently push the mix right into the tip) and pack it down so the bottom third is filled, approximately 1½in (4cm). Now take a marker pen, approximately ⅝in (15mm) in diameter with a flat end, and one or two gum strips cut from rolling papers. Push the flat end of the marker into the top of the smoking mix and pinch the paper around the marker as if you were making a Dutch Tulip. Wrap the gum strips around the paper-encased marker, at the point where the marker meets the smoking mix.

6 Remove the marker and use your fingers to open and uncrease any of the paper that has been crushed together in the previous step. Now fill the next third of the paper with smoking mix and pack it down so that it fills out the paper and forms a spherical shape. Insert the paper tube into the top of the smoking mix and pinch the remaining paper tightly around it.

7 Cut another one or two gum strips and use them to secure the tube in place. Give it a minute for any gum to dry and then it's ready to smoke!

Oompa-Loompa, doobie-dee-doo... I've got Double Bubble for you!!

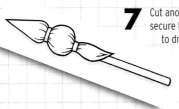

*Disclaimer: the rolling mix is not gooey, chocolaty, or everlasting; that was just said to keep up the Willy Wonka analogy.

T-BAR

Bin your bling, lose the lowrider, and ditch your gold grills… there's a new Pimp Daddy in town and its name is T-Bar. This badass mofo will get any party jumping and have everyone wanting to join you in this double dose of deluxe dopeness! The best bit is that it can be kept and used again and again!

1 Take two pieces of paper or thin card, approximately 6x2in (15x5cm). Roll them into two tubes, approximately the same diameter as a pencil but one slightly wider than the other. Seal them both with tape or rolling papers.

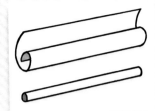

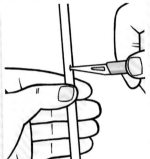

2 Use a sharp knife or scissors to cut a hole half way along the wider tube. The other tube will need to fit snugly into this hole, so be careful not to cut the hole too big. It is a good idea to start small and gradually increase the size of the hole until it is just right.

3 Insert the narrower tube into the hole and seal the junction with tape or gum strips removed from rolling papers.

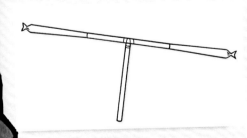

4 All that is left now is to roll two juicy joints, push them into each end of the T-Bar, and you'll soon have the party chanting your name like a true cheeba champion!

DEVIL'S TRIDENT

This menacing pitchfork of a spliff is known as a "Devil's Trident" because in order to survive one of these you will need to sell your soul to the devil! So get out your Ouija board, sacrifice a goat, and get ready for Beelzebub himself to appear in a flash of red smoke. Once you've parted ways with your eternal soul and put a Trident together, make sure Lucifer has a toke before he heads back down to Hell. Hopefully, you'll both forget why he came up to visit you in the first place!

1 Take two pieces of paper or thin card, one approximately 4x1½in (10x4cm) and the other 6x1½in (15x4cm). Roll them into tubes, making the shorter one slightly narrower than the other. Bear in mind that the longer tube needs to be a suitable diameter to insert a joint snugly into the end of it. Also, the shorter tube needs to be narrow enough to pass through the longer tube. Seal with tape or rolling papers.

2 Using a sharp knife or scissors, cut a hole about ½–⅝in (10-15mm) from each end of the shorter tube. These holes must only go through one side of the tube and not all the way through. They also need to be the right size for the roach end of a spliff to be inserted. Next cut a hole all the way through the middle of the tube.

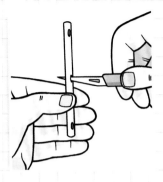

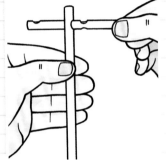

3 Now cut a hole all the way through the longer tube, approximately ¾in (20mm) from one end. Pass the shorter tube through it so that the center hole of the shorter tube lines up with the center of the longer tube. Make sure that air can clearly pass through.

4 Seal any gaps around the junction using tape or rolling papers. Also seal the open ends of the shorter tube.

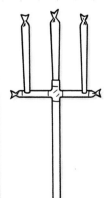

5 Insert joints into each of the three holes and invite two of your friends over to even up the numbers. Just be careful not to take someone's eye out whilst lighting up this bad boy!

MJÖLNIR

Named after Thor's very own hammer, this hard-hitting creation was forged straight from the flames of a Viking's furnace. As its name suggests, it'll hit you over the head and leave you seeing Norse gods flying through the sky for days. This thunderous big brother of the T-Bar is not for the faint-hearted and, once you've nailed it, you'll have Odin himself worshipping the ground you walk on.

1 To make this colossal creation you will need two pieces of paper or thin card, approximately 6in (15cm) wide: one should be about 8in (20cm) long; the other only needs to be about two-thirds as long (5in/12cm).

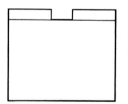

2 Take the longer piece and fold back about ½in (1cm) at one end.

3 Flip it over and fold back again. Repeat until you have made four folds to create a concertina effect.

4 Flatten it down and, using a sharp knife or a pair of scissors, cut out the middle section of the concertina.

5 Roll the remainder of the paper or card around this concertina so that it becomes enclosed within a tube. From one end of the tube the concertina of paper/card should look like an "M." This will prevent any smoking mixture from being knocked or sucked out of the tulip buds.

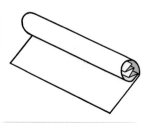

6 Seal this tube closed with tape or rolling papers and then roll and seal the other piece of paper or card into a slightly narrower tube.

7 Using the knife or scissors, cut a hole in the middle of the wider tube on the side that the top of the "M" touches. It needs to be just the right size for the narrower tube to fit into, so make sure you don't cut this hole too big. It is best to start small and gradually make it bigger if you need to.

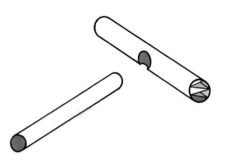

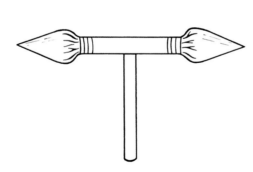

8 Wrap tape or rolling papers around the join to make sure it is airtight. Then make two tulips (see page 28) and attach them to each end of the wider tube; you can use gum strips or tie with thread.

Master this force to be reckoned with and there'll be a place waiting for you in the halls of Valhalla.

THAT'S DOPE!

The size of the wider tube made here is perfect for a standard two-paper tulip, but it can be made even bigger to accommodate larger tulips— if you are feeling brave enough!

A LITTLE PAUSE

After all that rolling and smoking, you'll no doubt be feeling a little stoned. Here are a few words of weed wisdom to think about while you build up the motivation to roll another joint...

"I used to smoke marijuana. But I'll tell you something: I would only smoke it in the late evening. Oh, occasionally the early evening, but usually the late evening——or the mid-evening. Just the early evening, mid-evening, and late evening. Occasionally, early afternoon, early mid-afternoon, or perhaps the late-mid-afternoon. Oh, sometimes the early-mid-late-early morning... But never at dusk."

Steve Martin

"Dope will get you through times of no money better than money will get you through times of no dope."

*Freewheelin' Franklin,
The Fabulous Furry Freak
Brothers' Comics*

"When you smoke the herb, it reveals you to yourself."

Bob Marley

"The illegality of cannabis is outrageous, an impediment to full utilization of a drug which helps produce the serenity and insight, sensitivity and fellowship so desperately needed in this increasingly mad and dangerous world."

Carl Sagan

"That is not a drug. It's a leaf."
Arnold Schwarzenegger

"It really puzzles me to see marijuana connected with narcotics, dope, and all of that stuff. It is a thousand times better than whiskey. It is an assistant and a friend."

Louis Armstrong

"They lie about marijuana. Tell you pot-smoking makes you unmotivated. Lie! When you're high, you can do everything you normally do just as well—you just realize that it's not worth the fucking effort. There is a difference."

Bill Hicks

BLUNT

You've completed the merger! You've won the case! You've sealed the deal! It's time to savor the moment and take a second to look out across the vast empire that you've built. This calls for a cigar… but with a difference. Kick back and ask your butler to fetch one of your finest Havanas before packing it to the rafters with sticky skunk. Due to the size of some of the cigars available, you may need a millionaire's bank balance to afford the pile of weed required to fill it!

1 To make a blunt you will need either a cigar or cigarello—the fatter the better, as it will give more width to the blunt paper and allow for easier rolling.

Although cigars are not particularly cheap, the more expensive and higher quality cigars will be made with higher grade tobacco leaves and ultimately lead to a superior blunt. Blunt wraps are available to buy, but they don't come close to the real deal and are best avoided. If your cigar has a closed end this must first be removed using a cigar cutter or a sharp knife. If the cigar has a label, this must also be removed.

2 Soak a small towel in warm water and then ring it out with your hands until no more water drips out. You want it to be damp but not overly wet. Now wrap the towel around the cigar for a few moments to moisten and soften it. You can also hold the cigar over the steam from a kettle or simply give it a good lick! Moistening the cigar can be repeated as much as is needed throughout, in order to keep it soft and prevent cracking.

3 Using a very sharp knife, start at one end and carefully cut down the full length of the cigar.

4 Insert a needle, toothpick, or any other suitable instrument into the cut and slide out the tobacco filling. It is best to remove a small section at a time, starting from the bottom and working up, so as to avoid damaging the outer layers.

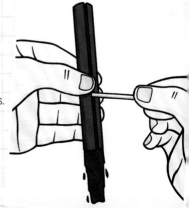

5 You will now have an empty cigar skin that can be laid out flat. Most cigars have an outer "wrapper" of a tobacco leaf wrapped around a thicker layer of reconstituted tobacco called a "binder." The binder is the part you want to keep, so, using your fingers, peel away the outer wrapper leaf.

6 Many blunt connoisseurs will insist that a true blunt should be made without a roach. It all comes down to personal preference and ultimately there is no right or wrong way to get stoned! However, using a roach will prevent the end becoming clogged with moisture and tar, and give you something to hold without getting your fingers burned. Despite the ongoing tobacco/no tobacco debate among joint smokers, most blunt tokers will agree that only pure weed or a weed-and-hash mix should be rolled up. However, a blunt can take quite a lot of filling so in hard-up times a little tobacco can be used.

7 Whereas joints are rolled by sliding the sides of the paper past each other to shape the mix and then using a tuck-and-roll technique, blunts aren't as workable and their size can be restrictive. Instead, the filling is pressed into place from above with your fingers and the blunt skin rolled and gently pressed to get the desired shape and density.

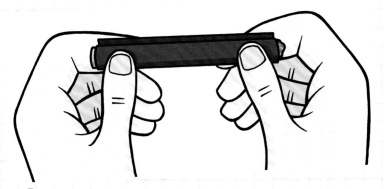

8 Once the weed is shaped sufficiently, use your thumb to tuck the front part of the blunt skin in behind the filling. Although there is no gummed strip, as on a rolling paper, lick along the inside of the flap, as you would with a rolling paper, and seal the blunt closed.

9 Finally, lick the blunt thoroughly all over to fully seal it, give it a tap and a poke, and leave for a few minutes to dry. If it is really wet, you can carefully run the flame from a lighter along the outside of the blunt to help it dry.

This is one for the special moments in life. Blaze up and blunt out. You deserve it!

HOLLOW JOINT

A joint with a hole in it! Why would anyone do such a thing? Well, because as masters of our art, we can. Like a stuntman driving a somersaulting motorbike off a cliff and landing on the tongue of a blue whale, it's difficult, it's impressive, and people will applaud us for it. Not that we love the spotlight but, as Reverends of Rolling, we need to give the world a little reminder of what we can do every now and then. Perfect this technique and you'll have those junior-jointers double taking at your mastery.

1 Cut a piece of paper to about the size of a king size rolling paper, approximately 4x2in (10x5cm). Roll it into a very narrow and tight cone and seal it together with sticky tape, making sure there are no sticky sections of tape facing outward.

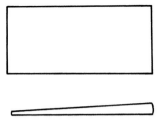

2 Lay this on a king size rolling paper with a small gap next to the narrow end and roll it up as if it were a joint. Try to roll it as tightly as you can.

3 Fold back the small section of empty paper at the narrow end and seal it closed with a piece of a gum strip removed from another rolling paper. Test to make sure that the paper cone can slide out of the rolling paper sleeve, but there is no need to remove it fully.

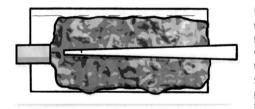

4 Lay a king size rolling paper flat out with the gum strip facing up and toward you and add an extra-wide roach. Spread out a thin layer of finely ground smoking mix all over the paper but not either side of the roach (as shown). You may find that pure weed works better for this roll, but if you do use tobacco make sure it is also ground up very finely with no hard lumps or sharp pieces. Lay the paper cone on top of the bed of weed, leaving a gap of approximately ½in (1cm) next to the roach.

5 Carefully pick up the paper so that the weed wraps around the paper cone, with a layer remaining intact underneath it. You will probably need to sprinkle some more smoking mix on top to give a complete and consistent layer.

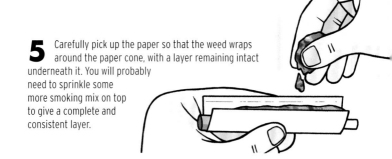

6 Now roll it just as you would a standard One-skin (see page 8), but trying to keep the weed in a complete layer around the cone. Once rolled, poke the weed down the gaps in the end of the joint with a narrow poker and top up with extra weed to bring it level with the end. Then slide the paper cone out from inside its rolling paper sleeve, making sure not to pull the rolling paper out with it.

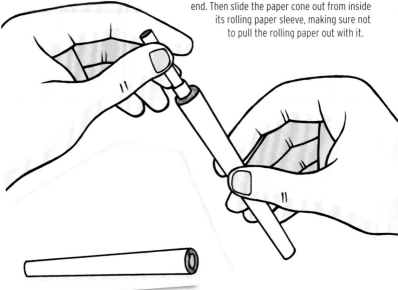

7 Trim any excess paper with a pair of scissors and give it a tap.

Now all that is left to do is step back, take a bow, and soak up the adulation!

TWISTER

Alert the storm chasers, batten down the hatches, and put on your mac; there's a storm a-brewing! Once you get this joint rolled, you'll have a natural disaster on your hands. This windy wonder is made up of three Two-skin joints that are braided together to form a triple-twisted spliff that will leave a trail of destruction in its wake! We would advise you to tie down your stash before attempting this roll as the weather patterns in your bedroom might get a little turbulent.

1 Although it is possible to use single length papers for a Twister, for a truly impressive creation a bit of extra length is needed. Rip-style papers are perfect for this; however, joining two king size papers together works just as well. To do this, use the technique explained in the Two-skin (see page 14).

2 Add a roach to the left-hand end of the paper and then add your smoking mix. Use your fingers to shape the mix into a fairly thin and even line.

3 Roll the joint fairly straight, even, and narrow. Due to the length you may want to rest one end on a raised surface while you work on the other end. If you are struggling to do this by hand, try using the Card Trick method (see page 63) but, instead of holding the paper in your hand, lay it down on a hard surface and use a ruler instead of a credit card. Alternatively, you could use a rolling mat. Tap the joint gently on a hard surface and give it a slight poke but do not twist it closed.

4 Roll two more joints in the same way, trying to make them as similar to each other as possible. Lay them out, side by side with the roaches lined up. Cut off the gum strips from two or three rolling papers and use them to bind the roach ends of the three joints together. Leave for a minute or two so that the gum strips are fully dry.

5 Take the joint from one side and pass it over the top of the middle joint so that they are snugly fitting together at the roach end. Then take the third joint and pass this over the one that is now in the middle. Again make sure they are fitting snugly together.

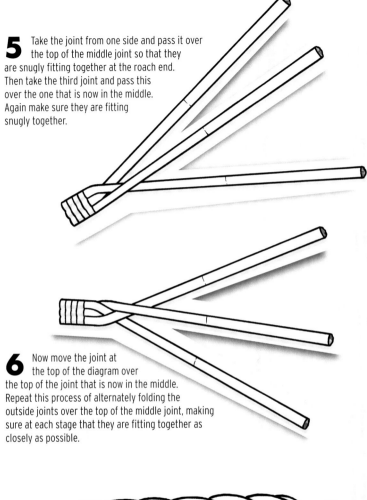

6 Now move the joint at the top of the diagram over the top of the joint that is now in the middle. Repeat this process of alternately folding the outside joints over the top of the middle joint, making sure at each stage that they are fitting together as closely as possible.

7 Once you have braided the full length of the joint, twist the three ends together and get ready to be blown away!

SCORPION

WARNING: this is a highly dangerous animal!
Handle with care!

This is Mother Nature at her finest. Roll this chronic creepy crawly and you won't know whether to smoke him or put him in a cage. To put it bluntly: this is one huge joint with three smaller ones pushed through to create the legs and two bigger ones for the arms; both topped off with tulip bud pincers… Get comfy, ladies and gentlemen, because this may a take a while.

1 To make the body of the Scorpion you will need four king size rolling papers. Lick the gum strip of one paper and stick it to the bottom edge of another paper. Then turn a third paper by 90-degrees and stick its gum strip to the right-hand edge of the first two papers. Be sure only to lick the area of gum strip that will be covered by the first two papers.

2 Fold up the bottom half of the lower horizontal paper and crease all the way along, through the vertical paper. Lick this crease and tear off the bottom part of the papers. Then take the fourth paper and stick its gum strip to the right-hand edge of the third paper, again only licking the section of gum strip that will be covered up.

3 Add a roach, plenty of smoking mix, and roll the joint as you would a Three-skin (see page 22) but with a second flap. Tap and poke the joint but not overly so, as some flexibility will be needed later.

4 Next, get five more king size rolling papers. Roll two cone shaped One-skin joints (see page 8) but without roaches and roll the other three papers into skinnier straight joints, also with no roaches. Twist both ends of the skinny joints but leave both ends of the cones open. Take a needle or other sharp pointed instrument and make a small hole (big enough for air to pass through) all the way through the center of the three skinny joints.

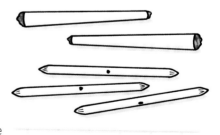

5 We now need to make two mini Dutch Tulip buds (see page 28), so take two more king size papers and stick the gum strip of one to the bottom edge of the other. Lick along the center crease line of the lower paper, tear off the

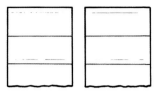

bottom section, and discard it. Now cut vertically through the center of the papers, splitting them in two.

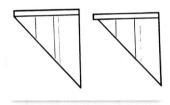

6 Fold the bottom left corner up at a 45-degree angle so that the edge lines up with the bottom of the gum strip. Without licking it, fold the gum strip down over the folded corner and run your finger along it to make a crease the full length of the paper. Fold back this crease slightly, lick the gum strip, and fold it back down so that it seals the folded corner. Repeat for the other section of rolling papers.

7 Cut or tear away the top part of both papers, as shown, so that the openings of the flattened tulip buds are level.

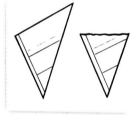

8 Open up these tulip buds and fill them with smoking mix, making sure to get it right in to the tips. Insert the conical joints (see step 4) into the tops of the smoking mix and pinch the paper around the stems of the joints to create the bud shapes. Secure the buds in place using the gum strips cut from a couple of extra rolling papers.

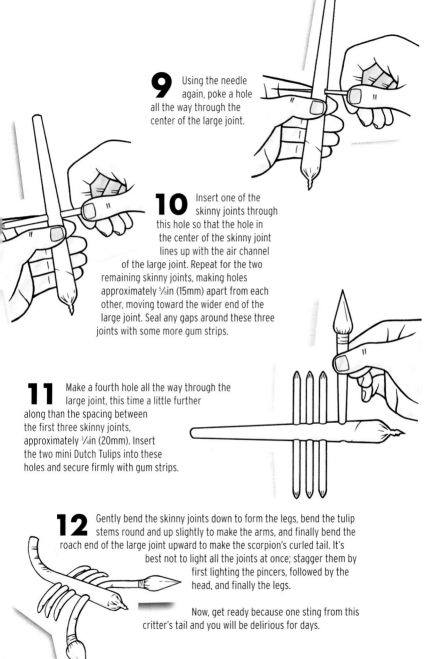

9 Using the needle again, poke a hole all the way through the center of the large joint.

10 Insert one of the skinny joints through this hole so that the hole in the center of the skinny joint lines up with the air channel of the large joint. Repeat for the two remaining skinny joints, making holes approximately ⅝in (15mm) apart from each other, moving toward the wider end of the large joint. Seal any gaps around these three joints with some more gum strips.

11 Make a fourth hole all the way through the large joint, this time a little further along than the spacing between the first three skinny joints, approximately ¾in (20mm). Insert the two mini Dutch Tulips into these holes and secure firmly with gum strips.

12 Gently bend the skinny joints down to form the legs, bend the tulip stems round and up slightly to make the arms, and finally bend the roach end of the large joint upward to make the scorpion's curled tail. It's best not to light all the joints at once; stagger them by first lighting the pincers, followed by the head, and finally the legs.

Now, get ready because one sting from this critter's tail and you will be delirious for days.

TECHNICOLOR DREAM SMOKE

Bring together two colored papers to create an eye-catching joint like no other! Mix and match until you find the right color scheme for any occasion, whether it's peacocking at a party or supporting your favorite team.

1 Take two different colored rolling papers and flatten them out with their gum strips facing up and toward you.

2 Cut away the bottom of one paper at an angle, then lick the gum strip of the uncut paper and stick it along the bottom cut edge of the first paper.

3 Using a sharp knife or scissors, cut away the bottom and right sides of the lower paper so that it is the same size and shape as an uncut king size rolling paper.

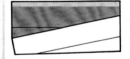

4 Fold the paper horizontally along the center to make a new crease line, unfold it, and lay it out as you would a standard joint with the gum still facing upward and toward you. Add a roach and your smoking mix.

5 Finally roll it in the same way as you would a One-skin (see page 8).

Smoke this and you'll feel like you've found the pot o' gold at the end of a rainbow!

CARD TRICK

Any type of credit card, playing card, ruler,
or rolling paper packet can be put to good use
in making a tightly rolled spliff. Magic!

1 Begin by preparing a rolling paper as you
would for a standard One-skin with a roach
and your smoking mix. As with a One-skin, slide the
back and front parts of the rolling paper back and
forth past each other to shape the smoking mix
inside into the desired baseball bat shape.

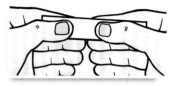

2 Rather than using the tuck-and-roll
technique, hold the paper in your left hand
so that the center crease of the paper is resting on
top of your middle finger, your index finger is
running along the back edge of the paper, and your
thumb is supporting the front.

3 Pick up a credit card in your right hand and push the
bottom edge of it into the front of the rolling
paper along the top edge of where the smoking mix is
inside. Move it back and forth from left to right along
the paper to compress the mix tightly into shape.

4 While moving the back-side of the paper up
slightly with your index finger, push the
card (and the front part of the paper) down
tightly behind the smoking mix.

5 Once the full length of the paper is tucked in
behind the mix, keep applying gentle pressure
on the joint with the left hand to prevent it unrolling
and slide out the card with your right hand. If you find
that you also need to use your right hand to hold the
joint together, you can use your mouth to pull out the card. Now lick the gummed edge
of the paper and use your thumbs to roll up the rest of the joint, sealing it closed. Give
the joint a gentle tap on a hard surface, poke the end, and give it a twist.

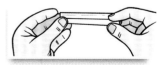

THANKS

Firstly, I would like to say a massive thanks to Pete for giving me the opportunity to write this book. It's been a lot of fun to write, even more fun making the joints (especially testing them!), and it's a privilege to be able to make a book that hopefully will be enjoyed by like-minded stoners around the world for many years to come. Also, thanks to Clare for editing, Paddy for your design work, and everyone else involved at Dog 'n' Bone Books.

A huge thank you as well to John for your inspired illustrations, I'm so pleased you were involved in the project; and to Phil for all your creative-writing help, you really saved the day.

I must say a special thanks to my mates Joe, Mehmet, Rat, and Adrian for being my smoking buddies all these years and for your help with this book (including all the testing!).

Some other people who deserve credit for making me the seasoned stoner and veteran roller that I am are: Sam (for having our first joints together all those years ago); Ben, Big Pete, Dave, Deano, Little Pete, Matt, and Mide (for three hazy years in Leeds); Will (for the one-flakes and everything else over the years); and Aydin (for the Starburst and everything else back in the day).

Also, shout outs to the following friends (hopefully they might buy a copy if their names are in this!): Christian, Gary, Mike, Robin, Steve, Sean, Savio, Amit, Willy, Natalie, and Justin.

Of course, I mustn't forget to mention my family: Mum and Dad; Tony, Chris, Helen and Sarah; and finally James, Katie, Amelia, and Dominic (you have all this to look forward to one day!).

If I've forgotten anyone, I'm sorry, I love you too; but it's 3am, I'm pretty stoned, and I don't have your number in my phone!

D